WHO WERE THE FRANKS?

Ancient History 5th Grade

Children's History

The Franks started with several Germanic tribes that had migrated from northern Europe to Gaul. That is where France currently sits. The name France comes from the name of the Franks. Two dynasties ruled over the Franks in the Middle Ages, the Carolingian Dynasty and the Merovingian Dynasty. Read further to learn more about the history and lives of the Franks.

MEROVINGIAN KINGDOM

The Franks became united first under King Clovis' leadership in 509 AD. The Merovingian Dynasty was founded by King Clovis and they ruled the Franks over the next 200 years. The Merovingian Dynasty name came from Clovis' grandfather, King Merovech.

King Clovis

King Merovech

Clovis and his Dynasty were victorious over the Visigoths, which forced them out of Gaul and over to Spain. He converted to Christianity and became the first King over the Franks to be recognized by the Pope as a king.

MEROVINGIAN MILITARY

The Frankish military incorporated many of the Roman institutions that were already in existence in Gaul, specifically during and following the conquests of Clovis I during the latter part of the 5th century and early part of the 6th century. The descendants of the Roman soldiers continued wearing their uniforms and performing the ceremonial duties throughout Gaul.

King Clovis and Clotilde

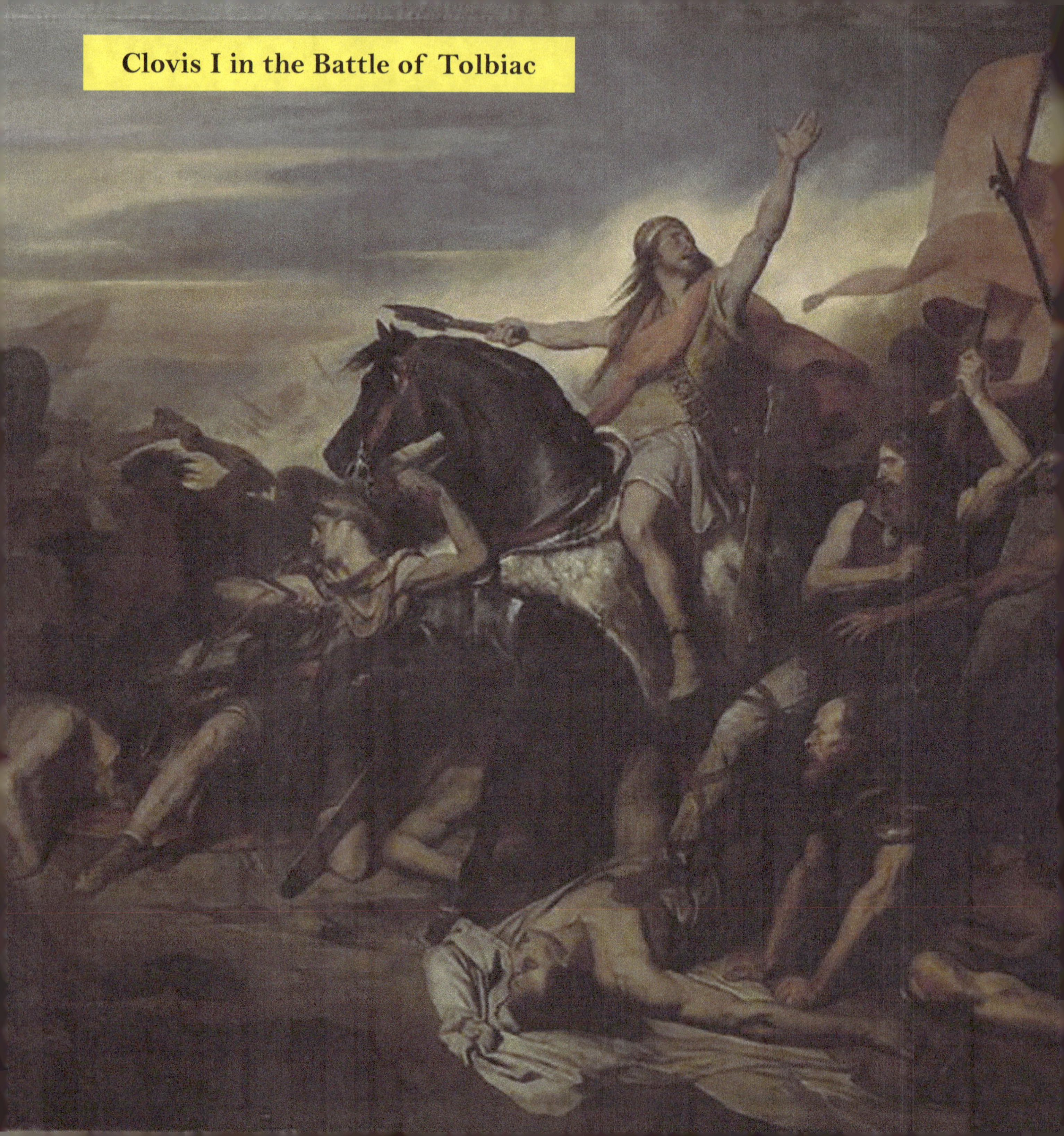
Clovis I in the Battle of Tolbiac

Just under the Frankish king were the leudes, his followers who typically were 'old soldiers' while serving away from court. Some of the historians have even gone as far as relating their taking of oath to the development of feudalism.

STRATEGY, TACTICS AND EQUIPMENT

Their armies used war horses, bows and arrows, swords, lances, shields, helmets, and coats of mail. Their society was militarized in nature. The Franks would call annual meetings each Marchfeld (March 1), as the king and his nobles would assemble in open fields and would determine their targets for the next campaign season.

Marchfeld

Rhine

These meetings showed strength of the monarch and was a way to retain loyalty within his troops. During their civil wars, the Merovingian kings would concentrate on the holding of places and using siege engines. During the wars against external enemies, the objective would typically be acquisition of booty or enforcement of tribute. Only beyond the Rhine did they seek to extend their political control.

Strategically, they would borrow greatly from the Romans, in particular with regard to siege warfare. Their tactics were flexible and designed to meet specific circumstances of a particular battle. The maneuver of subterfuge was utilized endlessly.

NORTH SEA

THE DANELAW

ENGLISH KINGDOM

London

chester

CHANNEL

FRIESLAND

Boulogne

Utrecht

LO 7 HA

Aix-la-Chapelle

Morsen

EAST FRANKISH

Hamburg

Bremen

Verden

SAXONY

Osnabrück

Minden

Magdeburg

Hildesheim

Münster

Paderborn

Halberstadt

Cologne

Fritzlar

THURINGIA

Hersfeld

Erfurt

Elbe R.

Slavic P

Oder R.

CARPATHIAN

Prague

MORAVIA

BOHEMIA

(Czechs)

KINGDOM

MORAV

Scheldt R.

Samport

Amiens

FRANCIA

Rouen

Kiersy

Ribemont

Soissons

Laon

Reims

Paris

Marne R.

Chalons

WEST FRANKISH

Le Mans

Chartres

Orléans

Sens

Fontenay

AQUITAINE

KINGDOM

Angers

Tours

Bourges

Autun

Limoges

Clermont

Toulouse

PYRENEES

SPANISH MARCH

Barcelona

Prüm

Treves

Verdun

Metz

Toul

Strasburg

Besançon

KINGDOM OF TRANSJURANE

Geneva

UPPER BURGUNDY

Lyons

Vienne

CISJURANE BURGUNDY

(ARLES)

Avignon

PROVENCE

SEPTIMANIA

Narbonne

Saracens

FRANCONIA

Fulda

Frankfort

Mayence

Worms

Würzburg

KINGDOM

Ulm

SWABIA

Lechfeld

(Field of Lies)

Basel

JURA MTS.

VOSGES MTS.

ALPS

ALPS

Aosta

Ivrea

KINGDOM OF

ITALY

Turin

Milan

Pavia

Po R.

Genoa

APENNINES MTS.

Constance

St. Gall

Coire

BAVARIA

Freising

Augsburg

Passau

Salzburg

Ratisbon

Danube R.

East March

Brixen

CARINTHIA

LOMBARDY

Trent

FRIULI

Treviso

Aquileia

Carniola

Verona

Venice

Drau R.

Save R.

CROATIA

DALMATIA

ADRIATIC SEA

Bologna

STATES OF

Ravenna

DUCHY OF SPOLETO

Ancona

Florence

Pisa

TUSCANY

Perugia

THE CHURCH

Spoleto

ITALY

Rome

Tiber R.

DUCHY OF BENEVENTO

Nice

CORSICA

To the Saracens, about the end of the 9th century

MEDITERRANEAN SEA

THE CAROLINGIAN EMPIRE

Once Pepin the Short took over power with support of the Frankish nobles, the Merovingian Dynasty came to its end. This was the beginning of the Carolingian Dynasty which ruled the Franks from 751 to 843.

The alliance attained by the Merovingians guaranteed the continuation of what became known as the Carolingian Renaissance. This Carolingian Empire became affected by internal warfare, but the combination of the Frankish rule and Roman Christianity ensured it was essentially united.

Carolingian Warrior

The Frankish culture and government was very dependent on each ruler and their goals and therefore each region of this empire became developed in different ways. Even though a ruler's goals depend on its political alliances within their family, Francia's leading families shared similar basic ideas and beliefs of government, having both Germanic and Roman roots.

CHARLEMAGNE

Charlemagne was the greatest to rule over the Franks and the Carolingian Empire, ruling from 742 until 814. He was also referred to as King Charles I or Charles the Great. He created both the German and French monarchies. He carried the nickname of "Father of Europe".

Charlemagne

Charlemagne receiving the submission
of Widukind at Paderborn in 785

He was able to expand the Frankish Empire to rule over a great part of Europe, but allowed local laws and cultures to remain. He would have the laws written and recorded, as well as ensuring these laws were enforced.

He was able to bring many reforms during his rule. One of these reforms was an economic reform which included establishment of the livre carolinienne, a monetary standard, rules on accounting, money lending laws, and control of prices by the government. He was also able to push for education and supported personally several scholars. He was also able to start schools in monasteries all over Europe.

Church Pope Adrian I
asks Charlemagne for help

The Coronation of Charlemagne by Raffaello Sanzio

Charlemagne impacted many different areas including the cultivation of church music, planting fruit trees, and civil accomplishments. An example of one of the civil works was building of the Fossa Carolina which was a canal connecting the Danube and Rhine rivers.

HOLY ROMAN EMPIRE

Charlemagne was crowned by the Pope as the first Holy Roman Emperor on December 25, 800 AD. This was the beginning of the Holy Roman Empire. As Holy Roman Emperor, he was considered as the guardian of the Catholic Church. He also now had backing of the church and was considered to be the leader of the monarchs of Europe.

Coronation of Charlemagne

Harun al-Rashid receiving a delegation of Charlemagne

This title was also held along with the rule over the Kingdom of Italy and the Kingdom of Germany. Theoretically, the Holy Roman Emperor was also primus inter pares, meaning first among equals, amongst the other Catholic monarchs. However, the Holy Roman Emperor could only be as strong as his alliances and his army.

AN EMPIRE DIVIDED

The unity that had been attained by the Merovingians guaranteed continuation of the Carolingian Renaissance. The Empire was affected by internal warfare, however, the combination of Roman Christianity and Frankish rule assured it remained united.

aurencius. de
xicolina. dux

Louis the Pious

After Charlemagne's death, Louis the Pious, his son, became ruler as the sole emperor. Louis had three sons and, according to the Frankish tradition, the empire was to be divided equally amongst the sons of the king. In 843, after King Louis' death, the Empire became divided in three states which later became countries such as France and Germany.

CULTURE

There were several ways in which the Franks became the heart of culture during the Middle Ages. They were responsible for development of the feudal and the knight system.

Coronation of Louis the Pious as king of Aquitane

Baptism Of Clovis I Sainted King Of The Franks

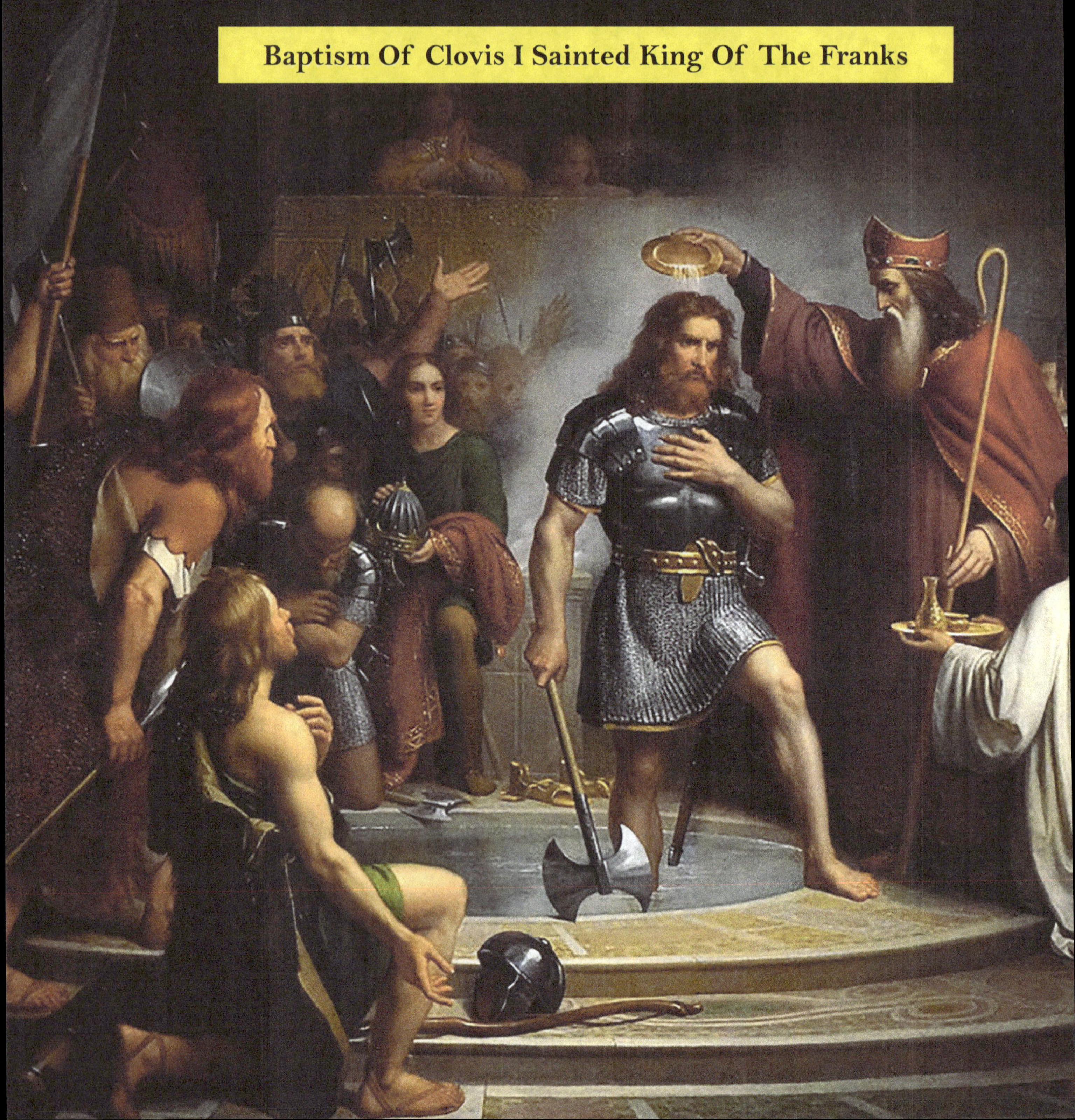

Once Clovis had passed away, many characteristics of the Frankish Kingdom, such as law, religious beliefs, and law became a mix of the Roman and Germanic cultures. They were also able to preserve many of the Roman industries and would apply Germanic craftsmanship in their architecture and art.

FRANKISH KNIGHT

The heavily armored cavalry was about the most powerful unit of the Frankish army. The soldiers soon came to be known as knights. Since the war horses and metal armor were very expensive, it was only the very rich that could afford becoming knights. The knights would then often be awarded land in exchange for their war services. This aided with development of the feudal system.

The Battle of Poitiers (1356)

Manor

FEUDAL SYSTEM

The feudal system was the basic society and government in Europe during the middle ages. Small communities formed around a local lord and manor. The lord would own the land and everything it contained. He would maintain safety for the peasants in exchange for their service. The lord would, in exchange, provide taxes or soldiers to the king.

Under this feudal system, land was divided between lords or knights. In exchange for land, the knights would pledge to fight. The land was referred to as a fief and both the title of knight and the land would often be inherited by the son that was the oldest.

Mer du Nord
Mer Baltique
DANEMARK
Neuendorf bei Wilster
Hambourg
BERLIN
PAYS-BAS
Magdeburg
Kassel
Düsseldorf
Elbe
BEL.
Francfort sur le Main
Rhin
LUX.
RÉPUBLIQUE TCHÈQUE
FRANCE
Stuttgart
Danube
Munich
AUTRICHE
Benrath Line

LANGUAGE

When they originally appeared during the 3rd century, they all spoke Proto-Germanic. By the 6th century, they would no longer speak the same language, with a phonetic change which was referred to as High German consonant shift, occurring along the north-south area (now known as the Benrath Line) that started the Low German in the north and High German in the south.

They are considered as descendants to the Rhinelanders who had a single language. Two language developed after the 6th century, Dutch and German. Once the Proto-Germanic period came to an end, the language became divided into different dialects, which included Frankish, also known as Franconian, and the predecessors of Saxon and Frisian. These dialects continued throughout the evolution of Dutch and German.

Clovis, King of the Franks, and his wife Clotilde

Childrens Crusade
Verulamium
Noviomagus
Caesariensis
Tricensimae
Novaesium
Londinium
Durovernum
Venta Belgarum
Dubrae
Noviomagus
Germania II
Atuatuca
Tungror
Gesoriacum
Augusta
Treverorum
Mogontiacu
Turnacum
Bagacum
Belgica II
Belgica I
Germania
Samarobriva
Divodurum
Rotomagus
Durocortorum
Argentorate
Augustodunum
GALLIAE
Constantia
Lugdunensis II
Lutetia
Parisiorum
Augustobona
Suindinum
Senones
Lugdunensis IV Senonia
Lugdunensis III
Aurelianum
Vesontio
Augusta Rauri
Turonum
Augustodunum
Maxima Sequanorum
Avaricum
Aventicum
Limonum
Lugdunensis I
Alpes Poenina
SEPTEM PROVINCIAE
(VIENNENSIS)
Genava
Octodurus
Lugdunum
Augustonemetum
Vienna
et Graiae
Mediolanium
Aquitania II
Aquitania I
Viennensis
Alpes
Burdigala
Vesunna
Segusio
Augus
Taurino
Valentia
Alp
Ebrodunum
Segodunum
Aquitania III
Aginnum
Arausio
Narbonensis II
Maritimae
Novempopulana
Nemausus
Lapurdum
Elusa
Augusta
Ausciorum
Tolosa
Arelate
Aquae Sextiae
Nicaea
Baetarnae
Massilia
Forum Iulii
Narbonensis I
Ompaelo
Narbo
ris
Emporiae
Osca
uriaso
Caesaraugusta
Ilerda
Barcino
Bilbilis
Tarraconensis
Tarraco

LITERATURE

Being situated within or surrounding Roman Gaul and across from Roman Britain, the Franks were the best educated, literarily prolific, and literate of the Germanics. The original Germanic cities were in their area. Many of the Franks held positions as high officers in the Roman administration. Their troops would guard the Romans from Britain to the Middle East.

Many documents were discovered within their territory, from tombstones to laws that were recorded on parchment. Their authors are the best sources of medieval history outside of the Gallo-Roman world. Old Frankish consisted mostly of oral communication, as far as we can tell from the writings that survived.

Gallo Roman Temple

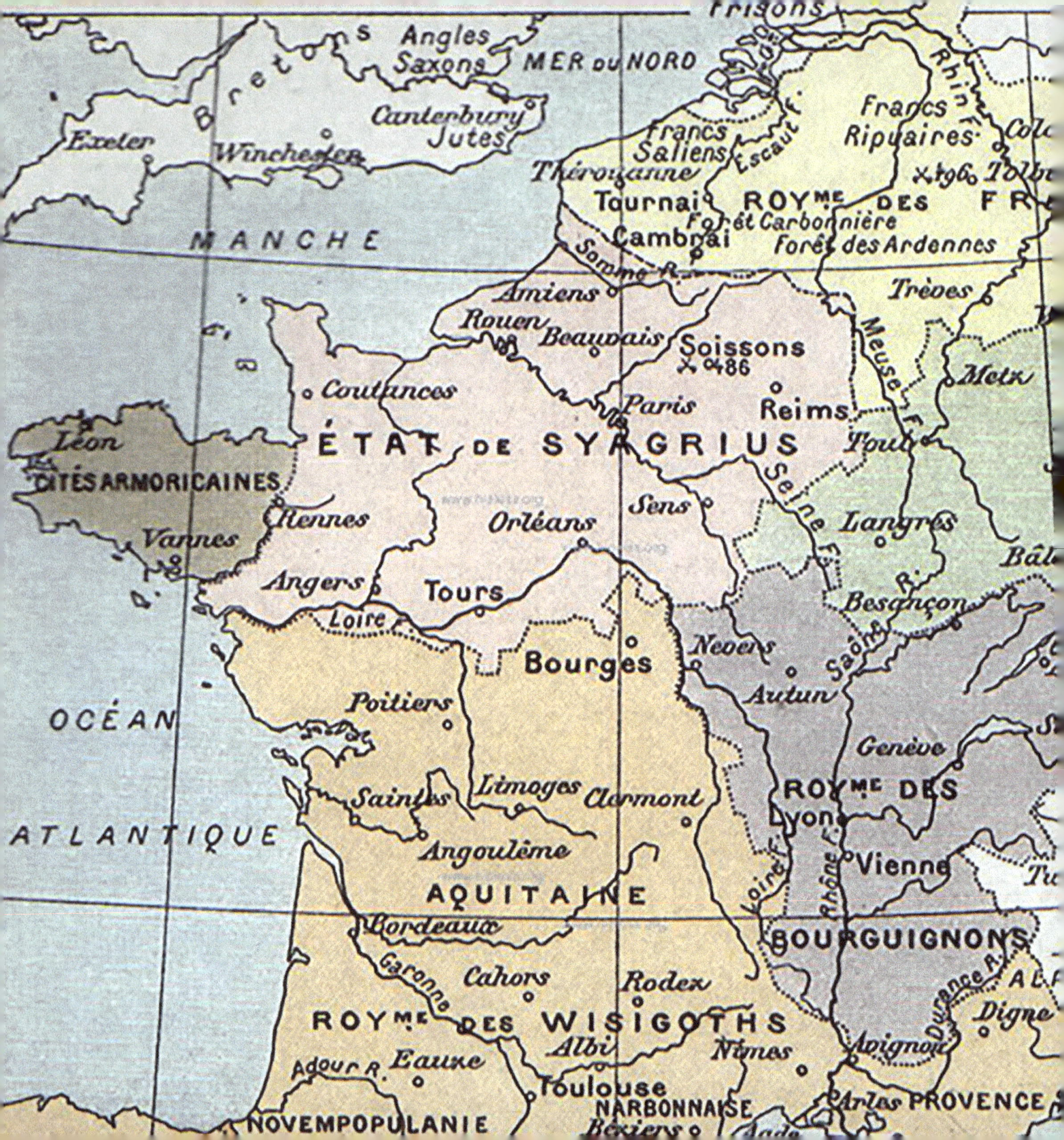

Bretons
Angles
Saxons
MER DU NORD
Frisons
Exeter
Winchester
Canterbury
Jutes
MANCHE
Francs Saliens
Francs Ripuaires
Escaut
Rhin R.
Col
Thérouanne
Tournai
Cambrai
Forêt Carbonnière
Forêt des Ardennes
×496 Tolbi
ROYME DES FR
Somme R.
Amiens
Rouen
Beauvais
Soissons
×486
Trèves
Meuse R.
Coutances
Paris
Reims
Metz
Léon
CITÉS ARMORICAINES
ÉTAT DE SYAGRIUS
Toul
Rennes
Orléans
Sens
Langres
Seine R.
Vannes
Bâle
Angers
Tours
Loire
Besançon
OCÉAN
Bourges
Nevers
Saône R.
Poitiers
Autun
Genève
ROYME DES
Lyon
ATLANTIQUE
Saintes
Limoges
Clermont
Vienne
Angoulême
AQUITAINE
BOURGUIGNONS
Bordeaux
Garonne R.
Cahors
Rodez
Durance R.
Digne
ROYME DES WISIGOTHS
Albi
Nîmes
Avignon
Adour R.
Eauze
Toulouse
NARBONNAISE
Arles PROVENCE
NOVEMPOPULANIE
Béziers
Aude

There appears to be no works of literature in the Frankish language, and they may have never even existed. The written language of Gaul was Latin prior to and during this period. Of any Gallic works which survived, there are some chronicles, several hagiographies and saints' lives, and a small number of poems.

Now that you have learned about the Franks, you may want to research additional information about their culture, language, and wars. You can do this by going to your local library, researching the internet, or asking questions of your teachers, family, and friends.

Visit

BABY PROFESSOR
EDUCATION KIDS

www.BabyProfessorBooks.com

to download Free Baby Professor eBooks
and view our catalog of new and exciting
Children's Books